The Prajñā-Sūtras: Aphorisms of Intuition

The Prajñā-Sūtras

Aphorisms of Intuition

Subhash Kak

DK PRINTWORLD
Publishers of Indian Traditions

Cataloging in Publication Data — DK

[Courtesy: D.K. Agencies (P) Ltd. <docinfo@dkagencies.com>]

Kak, Subhash, 1947- **author.**

The prajñā-sūtras : aphorisms of intuition / Subhash Kak.

pages cm

Includes sūtras in Sanskrit (Devanagari and roman).

"First published in India in 2007" – Title page verso.

Includes index.

ISBN 9788124604106 (PB)

1. Self-knowledge, Theory of. 2. Hindu philosophy. 3. Hindu cosmology. 4. Philosophy and science. I. Title.

LCC B132.S356K35 2025 | DDC 126 23

ISBN 978-81-246-0410-6

First published in India in 2007

Reprinted in 2025

Printed and published by:

D.K. Printworld (P) Ltd.

Regd. Office: "Vedaśrī", F-395, Sudarshan Park

(ESI Hospital Metro Station), New Delhi – 110015

Phones: (011) 4172 2626, 98713 94815

e-mail: indology@dkprintworld.com

Website: www.dkprintworld.com

Opinions

Subhash Kak has provided a brilliant original Sūtra text in the intuitive model of India's traditional yogic scholarship. He makes this ancient spiritual art of learning relevant to the contemporary man, showing us how to look beyond the boundaries of materialistic world to an inner view of both humanity and the universe in which there is a real understanding of the purpose of our lives.

David Frawley
author of *The Ṛg Veda and the History of India* and *Wisdom of the Ancient Seers*

The book strikes me as an excellent overview of Vedic conceptions, presenting them in a straightforward and transparent way that provides suggestive and clear insights for a modern reader. The science and the scholarship is well-founded and accurate, and the reasoning is simply presented without pretentious claims or obfuscating jargon. Given the depth and the delicacy of the subject, that's an uncommon and much-needed achievement. The use of Sanskrit terms is economical and illuminating, in a way that helps a modern reader to place them in the context of modern science and education.

Ananda Wood
author of *From the Upaniṣads,* and *Interpreting the Upaniṣads.*

Preface

THIS book is about the cosmology that underlines consciousness, written in the style of *sūtra*s. It considers questions such as freedom in a world bound by laws, the connection between the particular experience and the universal, art and its role, suffering and beauty.

The *sūtra*s are presented in their Sanskrit original, together with translation and commentary. The significance of these *sūtras* to questions of faith and meaning is also presented.

Baton Rouge,
January 7, 2007

Subhash Kak

Contents

Key to Transliteration

VOWELS

अ *a*	आ *ā*	इ *i*	ई *ī*	उ *u*	ऊ *ū*
(b<u>u</u>t)	(p<u>a</u>lm)	(<u>i</u>t)	(b<u>ee</u>t)	(p<u>u</u>t)	(p<u>oo</u>l)
ऋ *ṛ*	ए *e*	ऐ *ai*	ओ *o*	औ *au*	
(<u>rhy</u>thm)	(pla<u>y</u>)	(<u>ai</u>r)	(t<u>oe</u>)	(l<u>ou</u>d)	

CONSONANTS

Guttural	क *ka*	ख* *kha*	ग *ga*	घ *gha*	ङ *ṅa*
	(s<u>k</u>ate)	(bloc<u>kh</u>ead)	(<u>g</u>ate)	(<u>gh</u>ost)	(si<u>n</u>g)
Palatal	च *ca*	छ* *cha*	ज *ja*	झ *jha*	ञ *ña*
	(<u>ch</u>unk)	(cat<u>ch h</u>im)	(<u>j</u>ohn)	(hed<u>geh</u>og)	(bu<u>n</u>ch)
Cerebral	ट *ṭa*	ठ* *ṭha*	ड *ḍa*	ढ* *ḍha*	ण* *ṇa*
	(s<u>t</u>art)	(an<u>th</u>ill)	(<u>d</u>art)	(go<u>dh</u>ead)	(u<u>n</u>der)
Dental	त *ta*	थ *tha*	द *da*	ध* *dha*	न *na*
	(pa<u>th</u>)	(<u>th</u>under)	(<u>th</u>at)	(brea<u>the</u>)	(<u>n</u>umb)
Labial	प *pa*	फ* *pha*	ब *ba*	भ *bha*	म *ma*
	(s<u>p</u>in)	(<u>ph</u>ilooso<u>ph</u>y)	(<u>b</u>in)	(a<u>bh</u>or)	(<u>m</u>uch)
Semi-	य *ya*	र *ra*	ल *la*	व *va*	
vowels	(<u>y</u>oung)	(d<u>r</u>ama)	(<u>l</u>uck)	(<u>v</u>ile)	
Sibilants	श *śa*	ष *ṣa*	स *sa*	ह *ha*	
	(<u>sh</u>ove)	(bu<u>sh</u>el)	(<u>s</u>o)	(<u>h</u>um)	
Others	क्ष *kṣa*	त्र *tra*	ज्ञ *jña*	ळ* *ḷ*	ॠ* *ṝ*
	(*<u>kṣa</u>triya*)	(*<u>tr</u>iśūla*)	(*<u>jñā</u>nī*)	(*p<u>la</u>y*)	

अं (ं)*ṁ anusvāra* (nasalisation of preceding vowel) like *sa<u>ṁ</u>skṛti*

अः *visarga* = *ḥ* (aspiration of preceding vowel) like (*prāta<u>ḥ</u>*)

ऽ *Avagraha* consonant #'consonant (like:- *ime 'vasthitā*)

Anusvāra at the end of a line is presented by m (म्) and not ṁ

* No exact English equivalents for these letters.

1

Introduction

THESE *sūtras* came to me while I was on a Continental Airlines flight from Washington to Houston on October 13, 2002. I wrote them down very quickly, perhaps in no more than a few minutes. They encapsulate my intuitions on the essence of Vedic wisdom, and they could be useful in preparing oneself for the more complex texts of the tradition.

The previous night I had given a lecture at George Mason University in Fairfax, Virginia where the discussion at the end took a philosophical turn. I was struck by how our argumentation got bogged down in the attempts to sort out the defining terms, which were understood variously by different people.

In the Western tradition, this difficulty is mitigated by the fact that the concerns are generally regarding the outer aspects of things that are less contentious. Since Indian philosophy is concerned primarily with the experiencing self, its questions of definition are more troublesome. This is the reason why instruction in Indian philosophy is also given by employing synthesis that is based on stories. But it is a common error to take word (*śabda*) in its literal, surface sense as true cognition (*pramāṇa*). Much of contemporary academic scholarship has failed to sort through the different layers of the Vedic narrative by conflating the symbolic with the factual.

The *sūtra*s tie together some common symbols used in the Indian tradition to their deeper intuition. For someone who hasn't the time or the inclination to read the diverse texts of the Vedic tradition, they could serve as an introduction.

Why is *śabda* as literal word problematic? According to the tradition (as in the *Muṇḍaka Upaniṣad*), language can only communicate the lower form of knowledge, and true cognition is beyond words. From the point of view of language theory, the meaning of words is not determined objectively, for it must be fixed by context and other implicit information. Without a proper definition of words, a statement may be interpreted in different ways. Modern studies confirm the limitations of language and such limitations extend to other formal systems.

Taking the literal *śabda* as *pramāṇa*, we see commentators parse the great declarations (*mahāvākya*s) into contradictory interpretations. The same surface *śabda* may be interpreted as implying overlordship (*īśvaravāda*) by one group and reductionism (*nirīśvaravāda*) by another! Such enormous difference in meaning can lead to equally different approaches to reality.

Rather than the question of ontology, most people are interested in understanding themselves. There are questions like: Do we have a true self? According to the tradition, this self is the perceiving "I" who is independent of location and personal history, and this self is a unity. But how does one separate this core of one's being from the usual self who is known to us from our experience in space and time?

Sometimes, the image of the child, or even an infant, is used for the seeker in relation to Nature. Should the seeker have the attitude of the baby monkey who holds on to its mother, or that of the kitten, held by the cat by her teeth? The baby monkey as well as the kitten may be presumed to be in terror of falling, but there is more of an active role by the mother cat. These images are merely a means to intimate a structure to the projection of consciousness in our individual, conditioned selves.

From a practical point of view, one may avoid the problem of defining this structure by simply surrendering oneself to the inner self. But how do we recognize the innate spirit that we must surrender to? The problem is not any specific assertion (*vākya*), but rather the method of taking the literal word as the validation of a premise. The differences become ultimately an expression of different aesthetic attitudes. Underlying the process of knowing lies art.

Appreciation of art depends on the social experience of the individual and inherited tendencies. For example, my upbringing reinforced an ascetic aestheticism, a result of my parents' attitudes and circumstances, as also of the months we spent in literal isolation in our rooms in the long Kashmiri winter.

There exists an emotional angle to this question also. We are born with a feeling of mastery, but as we grow up we discover that things we desire are so desired by others as well. The experienced life is a contest of wills. Our failure in matching our expectations creates frustration, pain and disillusionment. We then use judgement and interpretation, provided by society or created by us, to explain why our desires cannot be met. The interpretation could have a basis in morality or magic, and we learn to see our childhood and the unfolding life through its lens.

Art represents new interpretive lenses that we have forgotten existed. It can be viewed as an escape from the habits of our own mind. But the art that we appreciate most readily is not radically different from our own modes of seeing. To appreciate art that is removed from our own necessitates a kind of awakening. An aesthetic attitude is a combination, in varying measures, of the different essences (*rasa*s) of it. It is one of the great insights of the Indian tradition that these essences are supposed to be discrete, and perhaps this idea emerged from the Vaiśeṣika atomic doctrine as well as the idea of Nyāya that mind operates sequentially. The basic *rasa*s are counted to be *śṛṅgāra* (eros), *hāsya* (humour), *karuṇa* (pathos), *raudra* (anger), *vīra* (heroic), *bhayānaka* (fearful), *bībhatsa* (odious), *adbhuta* (wondrous), and *śānta* (peaceful).

The feelings of fear and compassion are paramount as we reflect on how our ambition is thwarted by the fact that the whole world is against us. One often calls upon one's faith in a higher power or magic for rescue from this situation, passing from materialism to a belief in spirit. The recognition of the odds against oneself is a crisis that almost feels like annihilation, but it could also be a new beginning.

The seeker must be absorbed in the *vīra rasa* of the warrior. In the battlefield, theories of swordsmanship are pointless talk, any moment could be the last, and, therefore, he must be constantly awake to danger and opportunity from all sides. There is no time to dwell on any emotion but that of the immediate battle. This leads to a very austere perspective.

The Vedic tradition insists that *pratyakṣa*, direct perception, is the only way to validation. But it is the *pratyakṣa* of the inner experience (Advaitic or non-dual) and not that of its description in terms of the evolution of material processes. One can talk *around* it, but one cannot speak of this direct experience. This gap between true "understanding" and its description requires that one use various methods of logical inference (*anumāna*) and a proper enumeration of categories (*padārtha*) to obtain insight.

By moving away from material causes to fields, modern science has recognized new categories that make the process of inference of true cause somewhat easier than before. It is now possible, for example, to study brain processes that provide insight into the operation of personal consciousness. One may harness outer science to infer aspects of inner science even though the sciences of object and subject remain fundamentally apart.

The conundrums that remain are caused by the problem of change. The Vedic narrative does not describe "things," but rather transformations. However, our common sense cognitions are sequential, inscribing relations between objects. It is difficult to represent constancy in change, as in the history of flowers that blossom and fade away.

Some philosophers consider only linguistic problems to be worthy of study. But linguistic expressions ultimately are about things and objects and they cannot properly address the issues of the experiencing subject. Although everything can be reduced to known or knowable objects, the self cannot be so reduced.

Our normal experience is shaped by our habits of cognition (*saṁskāras*) that guide us between the polarities of world-cycle (*saṁsāra*) and extinction (*nirvāṇa*). The personal journey continues until one has reached a state where one transcends the fear of life and death, where *saṁsāra* and *nirvāṇa* become irrelevant. This state requires the burning away of one's own *saṁskāras*, to rise above the normal ways of seeing. The Vedic prayer for "immortality" is a prayer for this freedom, that liberates from the ordinary conditioned behaviour, which is a state seemingly beyond the noose of time.

But the Vedic way is more than a psychology to help us confront our fundamental aloneness by stressing our connections with all that surrounds us. If science is the collection of invariances that lie behind the ceaseless change of the phenomenal world, the Vedic system represents a science since it presents the cosmology that lies at the basis of the subjective self-finding objective truths.

It took me some time to decide whether these *sūtra*s should be called the *Vijñāna* or the *Prajñā-Sūtra*s. I originally picked *Vijñāna* but realizing that this word is now generally taken in the sense of formal knowledge, I believe *Prajñā-Sūtra*s is the better name. The subtitle, Aphorisms of Intuition, was suggested by my brother Avinash.

2

The Sūtras

1. बन्धुपरोक्षयज्ञाः विज्ञानस्य त्रिपादाः ।

bandhu-parokṣa-yajñāḥ vijñānasya tri-pādāḥ ।

The three feet of *vijñāna* are *bandhu, parokṣa,* and *yajña.*

2. देवभूतजीवात्मनोऽन्तरेण बन्धुः ।

deva-bhūta-jīvātmano 'ntareṇa bandhuḥ ।

Bandhus exist between the *devas*, the *bhūtas*, and the *jīvātman.*

3. मनसि प्रतिबिंबितं ब्रह्माण्डम् ।

manasi pratibiṁbitaṁ brahmāṇḍam ।

The universe is mirrored in the mind.

4. चिदाकाशस्य तदीयौ सूर्यचन्द्रौ ।

cidākāśasya tadīyau sūrya-candrau ।

The inner sky has its own sun and moon.

5. सूर्यचन्द्रावष्टोत्तरशतांशात्मकौ ।

sūrya-candrāv-aṣṭottara-śata-aṁśātmakau ।

One hundred and eight units characterize the sun and the moon.

6. सामान्य आधारितं ज्ञानम् ।

sāmānya-ādhāritaṁ jñānam ।

Knowledge is based on the universal.

7. शब्दः बन्धः ।

śabdaḥ bandhaḥ ।

Word associations lead to paradox.

8. भाषा अपरा ।

bhāṣā aparā ।

Linguistic knowledge is of limited kind.

9. विरुद्धानि इव अपि दर्शनानि परस्परपूरकानि ।

viruddhāni iva api darśanāni paraspara-pūrakāni ।

Darśanas, although seemingly contradictory, are com- plementary.

10. आन्तरिकस्थितयः परिसंख्यायोग्याः ।

āntarika-sthitayaḥ parisaṁkhyā-yogyāḥ ।

The inner states are countable.

11. भाषालोकविरुद्धाभासातीतं विज्ञानम् ।

bhāṣā-loka-viruddha-ābhāsa-atītam vijñānam ।

Vijñāna is beyond language and paradox.

12. यज्ञात् प्रज्ञा आविर्भवति ।

yajñāt prajñā āvirbhavati ।

Prajñā emerges out of *yajña*.

13. चित्तमाव्रियते वर्णैः ।

cittam-āvriyate varṇaiḥ ।

Colours (of changing hue) are the coverings of the mind.

14. पशुअसुरराक्षस आत्मनि निवसन्ति ।

paśu-asura-rākṣasa ātmani nivasanti ।

Animals, *asuras*, and *rākṣasas* reside within.

15. पशुत्वस्य नाशनम् एव मुक्तिः ।

paśutvasya nāśanam eva muktiḥ ।

Mukti is the vanquishing of the [inner] animal selves.

16. यज्ञो योगः परिणामः परिवर्तनं च ।

yajño yogaḥ pariṇāmaḥ parivartanaṁ ca ।

Yajña is *yoga*, which is becoming and transformation.

17. शरीरमनसि असम्भूतिसम्भूति अविद्याविद्ये पक्षाविव ।

śarīra-manasi asambhūti-sambhūti avidyā-vidye pakṣāviva ।

Body and mind, materiality and life, rules and understanding are like wings.

18. प्रज्ञा ऐश्वर्यं पक्षिणः उड्डयनम् ।

prajñā aiśvaryaṁ pakṣiṇaḥ uḍḍayanam ।

Prajñā is *aiśvarya* — the soaring of the [inner] bird.

Durgā Aṣṭamī Washington-to-Houston
13th October, 2002

3

Commentary

Now follows a short commentary on the *sūtras*. It puts each *sūtra* in an appropriate context.

1

बन्धुपरोक्षयज्ञाः विज्ञानस्य त्रिपादाः ।

bandhu-parokṣa-yajñāḥ vijñānasya tri-pādāḥ ।

The three feet of *vijñāna* are *bandhu*, *parokṣa*, and *yajña*.

Our knowledge is possible due to the mind's inherent capacity for it. It absorbs information and finds structure for doing so is its nature. Looking out, it creates a parallel world within. Its knowledge emerges from a familiarization with its inner space and it may be seen to be a consequence of the *bandhus* (bonds) that exist between the outer and inner worlds. If there were no such *bandhu*, it would be impossible to make sense of the world. Machines only follow pre-defined rules and they don't have *bandhus*, which is why they cannot be conscious. The *bandhus* are the ground that make awareness possible. The *bandhus* provide the answer to the question posed in *Kena Upaniṣad* 1.1:

केनेषितं पतति प्रेषितं मनः
केन प्राणः प्रथमः प्रैति युक्तः ।

केनेषितां वाचमिमां वदन्ति
चक्षुः श्रोत्रं क उ देवो युनक्ति ॥

keneṣitaṁ patati preṣitaṁ manaḥ
kena prāṇaḥ prathamaḥ praiti yuktaḥ ।

keneṣitāṁ vācam imāṁ vadanti
cakṣuḥ śrotraṁ ka u devo yunakti ॥

By whom directed does the mind fall (upon objects)?
By whom yoked does the first vital air move?
By whom wished are these words spoken?
Which god unites the eye and ear (with the objects)?

The outer world is infinite in size and relationships, and it appears that the inner world has infinite potential. These two worlds of object and subject arise from a single reality. Language can deal effectively with outer objects and their associations, and it is limited in its ability to provide complete subjective insight. True meaning must transcend linguistic description. Ordinary knowledge is objective whereas deepest knowledge concerns the subject, the experiencer. No wonder that personal language-based knowledge turns out to be paradoxical (*parokṣa*) at the intersection of different formal categories.

Perfect clarity is impossible in the phenomenal world not only because of the limitation of our senses, but also if it were to exist, it would paralyse the will. *Parokṣa* is the veil that makes the world interesting, and possible. The subjective self follows its nature, which is to be like the universal self, which is to be as large and great as it can be. As the *Bṛhadāraṇyaka Upaniṣad* (4.5.6) says:

न वा अरे सर्वस्य कामाय सर्वं प्रियं भवत्यात्मनस्तु कामाय सर्वं प्रियं भवति ॥

na vā are sarvasya kāmāya sarvaṁ priyaṁ bhavatyātamanastu kāmāya sarvaṁ priyaṁ bhavati ॥

Everything is not dear that you may love everything
But that you may love the Self, therefore everything
is dear.

It is from self-love that desire to power rises. This desire gets embodied in the will. But this will is distorted by our frustrations at not getting our desires fulfilled.

Our physical nature binds us to the processes of creation and destruction. Just as we have the instinct to master and create, we also have the instinct to destroy what is hindering our progress.

Often, people adopt values whose effect is to diminish them. They do so because they have embraced false magical theories in the hope that something good will come out of it in the end. In the most extreme of these theories, the good comes out only at the end of this life, in paradise.

The perception of time in our minds is the basic fabric of reality. The continuing change around us compels us to confront nature and we do it in a variety of ways that reflects our unique experience in life.

We play out the movements taking place in front of us. Man is a mimic animal, happiest acting a part, needing a mask to tell the truth. The core within has no form. There is a superposition of several persona in the background, projected serially on the different planes of the self.

The human face projects the complexities and paradox of the inner being. It is a juxtaposition of several, just as reality is a juxtaposition at any moment of several histories. The gods have multiple faces.

The ordinary *pratyakṣa* of material relationships and its description by language freezes "understanding" to that of surface processes and one must reach for a deeper *pratyakṣa*. Modern technology has made it possible to see, through a process of inference (*anumāna*), layers of reality that are much deeper than was possible with pre-modern materialist science. Nevertheless, the seer remains outside the scope of such science.

Yajña is sacrifice, a process that leads to transformation, implying that higher states exist. The performance of *yajña* makes renewal possible. As sacred theatre, it need not be done on an outer stage, but it may also be performed internally. Each performance changes the subject. The mystery of life and *yajña* is the mystery of time and change.

Transformation entails an abandonment of the earlier. It may be seen as a ritual rebirth. According to Mahidāsa Aitareya in the *Aitareya Brāhmaṇa* 1.3:

> पुनर्वा एतमृत्विजो गर्भं कुर्वन्ति यं दीक्षयन्ति ।
> *punarvā etamṛtvijo garbhaṁ kurvanti yaṁ dīkṣayanti* ।
> Whom they consecrate, the priests make into an embryo again.

The three feet of *bandhu*, *parokṣa* and *yajña* are like the triple categories of the sun, earth, and the atmosphere that provide structure to our physical experience, and that of the mind, body, and breath of our inner experience. They may also be compared to the states of dreamless sleep, waking and dreaming.

The *bandhu* makes the world knowable, *parokṣa* endows it with mystery, and *yajña* is the doorway to inner understanding. The veil of *parokṣa* is *māyā*, which shines through as the power that underlies reality. If outer science is concerned about laws (*ṛta*) relating to physical reality, our personal experience concerns choices. *Māyā* is the bridge between the laws of the outer and the freedom of the inner.

The *bandhus* represent the laws that hold the universe together (Viṣṇu), *parokṣa* is the dance of consciousness that is ever-changing (Śiva), and *yajña* is the process of change (Devī).

When seen as the agency of change, we have the Devī described thus (*ṚV* 10.125.8):

> अहमेव वातइव प्र वाम्यारभमाणा भुवनानि विश्वा ।
> परो दिवा पर एना पृथिव्यैतावती महिना सं बभूव ॥
>
> *aham eva vāta iva pra vāmy ārabhamāṇā bhuvanāni viśvā* ।
> *paro divā para enā pṛthivyaitāvatī mahinā saṁ babhūva* ॥
>
> Creating all these worlds, I move like air. My greatness is such that I am greater than the heavens and the earth.

The fourth foot of *vijñāna* is *pratyakṣa* of the direct experience. But it is subjective and it cannot be communicated through language. Nevertheless, without it there can be no intuitive understanding. According to *ṚV* 10.71.5, अधेन्वा चरति माययैष वाचं शुश्रुवां अफलामपुष्पाम् *adhenvā carati māyayaiṣa vācaṁ śuśruvāṁ aphalāmapuṣpām*, one who does not know the right meaning is like one listening to fruitless, flowerless sound, which is like possessing a fake cow for its non-existent milk.

In a similar manner, Yāska says in *Nirukta* (1.18):

स्थाणुरथं भारहारः किलाभूद् ।
अधीत्य वेदं न विजानाति योऽर्थम् ॥

sthāṇuratham bhārahāraḥ kilābhūd ।
adhītya vedam na vijānāti yo 'rtham ॥

One who reads the Veda but does not know its meaning is like a draught animal.

Clearly, the idea of knowing the Veda is not merely to read it, but to understand its meaning in one's heart. This is paradoxical, since one cannot understand the text unless one has already had the experience of its deepest intuitions. The text of the Veda cannot in itself be used for instruction.

2

देवभूतजीवात्मनोऽन्तरेण बन्धुः ।

deva-bhūta-jīvātmāno 'ntareṇa bandhuḥ ।

Bandhus exist between the *devas*, the *bhūtas*, and the *jīvātman*.

There are many levels of connections, some of which are direct whereas others are more subtle. The most direct are the ones described by physical or temporal proximity; the more subtle ones are connected through long chains of contact and by non-material forces.

The *bandhus* existing between the physiological and physical (astronomical) processes are the basis of biological cycles. There are other similar connections between the cognitive centres of the mind (*devas*) and the lights in the sky, pointing to cycles in psychological processes.

Bandhus exist across space, scale, and time. They cause patterns to be repeated in large and small structures and at different times. *Bandhus* might appear like silken bonds, but they tie stronger than iron chains.

The small leads to the intermediate, and together they lead to the large. Their properties are mutually related.

The recursion across space and time means that there is no unique reference and spirit (as the perceiving self) exists across forms. The body is like the wife to the spirit. The two must cohabit to create new forms, but the pleasures of the two rarely coincide.

The *Puruṣasūkta* tells us that the mind runs by the cycle of the moon whereas the sight works by the cycle of the sun. The science of biological rhythms bears this out. Experiments on volunteers who lived in caves showed that they tended to wake 50 minutes later every day, in agreement with the moon cycle of about 24 hours and 50 minutes.

There exist different kinds of clocks in the cells of the body. Harmonizing of physiological and psychological processes leads to a recognition of inner states. When one lets go, it is easier to be oneself.

Our usual sense of symmetry comes from the horizontal symmetry of the face; but there exist other symmetries, including one across scale.

The physical universe has recursive structures. These show up in similar patterns across scale and time, a consequence of the *bandhus*. Cyclicity is universal.

The world is a connected whole. Consisting of diverse forms of life, nature is a web. The knots of beings hold the net of life together. The strength of the net depends on the integrity of all the knots.

To make sense of the inner world, one path is to explore the complex web of *bandhus* of the outer world. Inference (*anumāna*) may be used in new ways.

The senses have *bandhus* amongst them as well. Full awareness is essential to transcend them.

The traces left by change flow out like ripples on water, and the ripples bounce back.

According to Patañjali,

> दृष्टदृश्ययोः संयोगो हेय हेतुः ॥
> *dṛṣṭadṛśyayoḥ saṁyogo heya hetuḥ* ॥
>
> The conjunction of the knower and the knowable is the cause of pain. — *Yoga-Sūtra* 2.17

The *bandhus* have the capacity to liberate as also to cause sorrow. In addition, there exist "false" *bandhus* projected by the mind: (विपर्ययो मिथ्याज्ञानम् अतद् रूप प्रतिष्ठम्) *viparyayo mithyājñānam atad rūpa pratiṣṭham*, false cognition is the knowing of the unreal, not possessing its own form (*Yoga-Sūtra* 1.8).

When false *bandhus* are accepted, the effect is confusion. Instead of pursuing a path which will further understanding, it becomes the path of diminishment. Under the influence of false "magical" ideas, one is prepared to suspend one's own judgement for the assertions of another. One may even accept that universal laws are ushered in by this prophet or the other.

3

मनसि प्रतिबिंबितं ब्रह्माण्डम् ।

manasi pratibiṁbitaṁ brahmāṇḍam ॥

The universe is mirrored in the mind.

The mirroring of the universe in the mind is the ultimate assertion of the bond between the inner and the outer. This forms the basis of the assertion that the universe is "knowable." This mirroring is not merely the representation created by the mind of the outer world, it offers a more fundamental connection between the subjective and the objective worlds. The mirroring is the key to the mystery of knowledge and awareness.

The universe must include both the material world as well as the collection of all minds. But it cannot be described only at one moment and then seen as evolving from one form to another. If it did, then the mind would be only a sequence of snapshots. As *Muṇḍaka Upaniṣad* 1.2.12 informs us:

> परीक्ष्य लोकान कर्मचितान् ब्राह्मणो ।
> निर्वेदमायान्नास्त्यकृतः कृतेन ॥
>
> *parīkṣya lokān karmacitān brāhmaṇo* ।
> *nirvedamāyānnāstyakṛtaḥ kṛtena* ॥
>
> Having examined worldly experiences and works, the wise
> Learn that the uncreated (limitless) cannot be produced by action.

The limitless universe is the *Brahman*, defined in *Taittirīya Upaniṣad* 3.1.1 thus:

> यतो वा इमानि भूतानि जायन्ते । येन जातानि जीवन्ति ।
> यत्प्रयन्त्यभिसंविशन्ति । तद्विजिज्ञासस्व । तद्ब्रह्मेति ॥
>
> *yato vā imāni bhūtāni jāyante yena jātāni jīvanti* ।
> *yat prayantyabhisaṁ viśanti* । *tadvijijñāsasva* । *tad brahmeti* ॥

From which all these elements emerge
By which, those born, are sustained
Unto which they enter at their end
Understand that to be *Brahman*.

If we can make sense of the universe, then *ayam ātmā brahma* (अयम् आत्मा ब्रह्म), the *ātman* is *Brahman*. This mirroring makes it possible to obtain knowledge by looking within. This knowledge emerges from a convergence of the outer and inner. Awareness of consciousness deepens understanding of both psychology and physics.

The mirroring of the universe implies that within each individual lie elements of all oppositions such as male and female, possessor and sacrificer, the hero and the knave, the *deva* and the *asura*.

Since the oppositions complete each other, the outer of one form has the opposite of it immmediately within, in sequence. Thus the male typically has an outgoing sense of self, a receptive field of emotion, an outgoing mind, a receptive field of intuition, and an outgoing field of bliss; for the female, the sequence is reversed.

The mirroring further means that a division of knowledge into analytic (obtained by logic) and synthetic (obtained by experiment on matter) is not correct, because each of these depends on the other.

But the mirroring does not mean that the world is transparent, due to the curtain of *parokṣa*. This curtain provides a structure on a reality in which the only constant is change.

This mirroring is the reason behind the need for individual integrity. An ethical basis that embraces all creation provides a unity to the reflection. Without such a basis one is atomized into many mimic selves.

Mind appears to have a surface which conceals a complex body. The angularities created by the surface have their own underside. What appears to be missing is what the mind craves.

Mind is a fire that burns, it is not a vessel of information. The fire consumes and transforms and presents the things around it in different lights.

Perfect accuracy of thought is unattainable. Our mental dance has much freedom in it. To the less intelligent the world appears quite sensible in its appearance; to the most aware also it is sensible. It is those in the middle who are most perplexed.

There are two ways of exploration: the outer to inner, and the inner to outer. In practice, one needs to use one as a reference to proceed to the other. Therefore, movement in outer and inner goes hand in hand.

The mind is in constant dialogue, reflecting on the outer in its past and the extrapolated future. The dialogue can be a recounting of images or feelings, or it can be their verbal representation. The verbal dialogue begins with words used in simple association of feelings and images but, later, upon deeper reflection, it raises the question of the "meaning" of words.

For example, what does "I" mean? Does it mean my body (which is subject to continuing change from age, disease, injury and so on) or my psychological self (which is also changing since the mind can be more "aware" sometimes than at others)? It is surely not the body alone because when the mind is extinguished the body dies as well. Neither is it the self alone, as a machine with a "mind" (should that ever come to pass) will not quite be an individual in the same sense as us humans. Likewise, what is love? Is it a feeling to own, dominate, teach, share, sacrifice? Or is it many things based on context? What is ownership? Learning? Knowledge?

Reflection on each of these leads to the understanding that no term can be defined in an absolute sense. Each meaning is the projection of an unstated narrative, defined in terms of a scene, a succession of images.

We realize that word meanings are not primary, being secondary to image narrative. This squares with the view that language comes later than sight (outer, inner, and both). Sight, in itself, comes after feeling of comfort or distress superimposed on a binding with the image of the universe.

When the mind grasps the universe, the senses retreat. In this state, one hears and sees with the mind and not with the ear and the eye.

4

चिदाकाशस्य तदीयौ सूर्यचन्द्रौ ।

cidākāśasya tadīyau sūrya-candrau ।

The inner sky has its own sun and moon.

The mirrored universe of the mind has a structure that parallels the outer universe. This paralleling is more than an inner representation of the outer; the inner world is dynamic with its own sun and moon, the primary and reflected lights of the mind.

The physical body also has aspects that correspond to the sun and the moon: there are physical processes that run by the two times. Also, the inner self is like the sun and the subjective self which associates itself with personal experience is like the moon. The personal self obtains its illumination from the inner self.

The inner moon is forever apart from the sun. Their images only appear to be together, as in an eclipse. Our inner life has a duality associated with it that comes through in our inner dialogue.

The body moves with the moon; the order is that of the sun. This basic dichotomy fashions not only our inner life, but also social organization.

The primary and the reflected lights provide a shading for the continuing dialogue within. They help to shift the focus from one to the other.

For the individual, the two hemispheres of the brain are the ground for the continuing dialogue. But within the brain are other binaries that partake of this dialogue at other levels.

Just as explorations of the outer are helped by using the light of the outer sun and the moon, the exploration of the inner are facilitated by the recognition of the two inner lights.

To know the outer, one must first explore the inner world. These two worlds cannot be kept apart. But to know the inner, it is essential to become familiar with the outer.

The process of exploration changes the inner and helps one find a proper measure of one's self. One is able to discover the structures within.

To know the outer, one must use all the inner senses:

including those that become available through the process of *sādhanā*.

The mind's response begins before the conscious mind adopts it as its own. This is the beginning of rationality and order. The conscious may censor and deny, but it will recognize the truth when shown.

The outer is created by the inner. Reality is a projection of the perceiving self. The Self joins the outer and the inner as in *Kena Upaniṣad* 1.2:

> श्रोत्रस्य श्रोत्रं मनसो मनो यद् ।
> वाचो ह वाचं स उ प्राणस्य प्राणः चक्षुषश्चक्षुः . . . ॥
>
> *śrotrasya śrotraṁ manaso mano yad* ।
> *vāco ha vācaṁ sa u prāṇasya prāṇaḥ cakṣuṣaścakṣuḥ* . . . ॥
>
> It is the ear of the ear, the mind of the mind, The speech of speech, the life of the vital air, It is the eye of the eye.

The mystery of the mirroring is thus inherent in the mystery of the power of the sense organs. They are mere instruments and without the conscious self behind them they cannot function. But consciousness does not simply transcend the mind; it pervades everything.

The inner sky is a projection of the transcendental self, unconstrained by space and time. As in *Kaṭha Upaniṣad* 2.5.15:

> न तत्र सूर्यो भाति न चन्द्रतारकं
> नेमा विद्युतो भान्ति कुतोऽयमअग्निः ।
>
> तमेव भान्तमनुभाति सर्वं
> तस्य भासा सर्वमिदं विभाति ॥
>
> *na tatra sūryo bhāti na candra tārakaṁ*
> *nemā vidyuto bhānti kuto 'yam agniḥ* ।

tameva bhāntamanubhāti sarvaṁ
tasya bhāsā sarvamidaṁ vibhāti ॥

There the sun shines not, nor moon and stars
Nor lightening, much less fire
You alone shine and everything shines after you
By your light all this is lighted.

The sun and the moon of the inner sky cannot be seen directly; we can only see with them. *Kena Upaniṣad* 1.3 says:

न तत्र चक्षुर्गच्छति न वाग्गच्छति न मनः ।
न विद्मो न विजानीमो यथैतदनुशिष्यात् अन्यदेव तद्विदितादथो . . . ।

na tatra cakṣur gacchati na vāg gacchati na manaḥ ।
na vidmo na vijānīmo yathaitad anuśiṣyāt anyad eva tadviditādatho . . . ।

The eye does not reach there, nor speech, nor mind.
Nor do we know (its nature). Therefore we don't know how to teach it.
It is other than the known and distinct from the unknown.

Seeing the inner world from "outside" is made possible by the illumination of *Brahman*.

5

सूर्यचन्द्रावष्टोत्तरशतांशात्मकौ ।

sūrya-candrāv-aṣṭottara-śata-aṁśātmakau ।

One hundred and eight units characterize the sun and the moon.

There are patterns in the outer world. The material has an atomic base, therefore number is basic in the formation of the world. From numbers emerge patterns and symmetries that are the basis of beauty.

The sun and the moon are about 108 times their respective diameters away from the earth. Furthermore, the sun diameter is about 108 times the earth diameter. The actual distances are:

Equatorial diameter of the earth: 7,926 miles
Mean diameter of the moon: 2,160 miles
Mean distance between earth and moon: 238,857 miles
Mean diameter of the sun: 864,000 miles
Mean distance between earth and sun: 92.9 million miles

Since the relative distance in relation to the diameter is the same for the sun and the moon, they look about the same size from the earth.

This unique measure is reflected in our inner sky and, therefore, inner states cannot be spanned instantaneously. Due to the vastness of the inner sky, we need time to transition from one state to the other. It is to make steady the exploration of the inner that certain *mantra*s are repeated 108 times.

Since the outer sun is mirrored into the inner sun, the location of the inner light will be at a point of focus characterized by the inverse of the number 108. Thus the self appears small, hidden in the cave of the soul, even though it is immense.

The nature of our understanding is a function of the size and nature of our outer and inner worlds. Nature is perfect not only in its biological machinery but also in the size that makes it possible for us to conceive of and comprehend it.

The structure of the perceiving self reflects measures of the outer world. This is what makes the Vedas more than a psychology.

Laws have a numerical basis also because of mind's tendency to classify, leading to numerical categories. Mind's seriality and the atomicity of matter are complementary properties.

Numbers make it possible to distinguish man and beast, noise and rhythm, movement and dance. Numbers help us find the boundaries within of different regions. This unveils inner structure, showing that much of the inner is an extension of the outer.

The measure of the universe is beauty and its experience is an unveiling that is like a discovery of self.

6

सामान्य आधारितं ज्ञानम् ।

sāmānya-ādhāritaṁ jñānam ।

Knowledge is based on the universal.

Knowledge is universal, independent of the subjective self. Hence the statement, *prajñānam brahma* (प्रज्ञानं ब्रह्म), intelligence is *Brahman*.

Since knowledge can only be defined with respect to intelligence, this sets up a circular relationship between the self and the material world. The universality of knowledge comes with a paradox at its basis.

Knowledge springs from the heart and wisdom is in its unfolding. When it comes to emotion, it is easy to see how we are connected. It is to feel the universal, to go from the particular experience of oneself to that of every man, that one likes to hear and read stories. No wonder that bliss — the feeling of oneness with the world — is considered higher than intuition and that it is considered the doorway to deeper knowledge.

Nature appears to be blind, driven by the exertions of the many individual selves in their own cycles of growth and decay. The large patterns of change become apparent only in retrospect.

Our behaviour is mostly reflexive driven by our nature. We have access to our intelligence only at *samādhi*, or moment of peak experience. At *samādhi*, our physical boundaries dissolve and we melt into a larger presence which expands and we seem to fill all we behold.

The basis of the universe is in knowledge. Information is the most valuable resource for discovery of patterns across time. By virtue of its large changes, it makes clear that the belief in a material ground is not quite true.

The natural or cosmic laws (*ṛta*) are the ground on which the physical world rests.

Laws come first. The material world emerges later. But laws have no meaning without reference to the material world.

The state in which the universal is recognized is *Īśvara*. According to Patañjali:

क्लेशकर्मविपाक आशयैः अपरामृष्टः पुरुष विशेष ईश्वरः।
kleśa karma vipāka āśayaiḥ aparāmṛṣṭaḥ puruṣa viśeṣa īśvaraḥ ।

> *Īśvara* is the unique self untouched by the vehicles of affliction, action and fruition. — *Yoga-Sūtra* 1.24

7

शब्दः बन्धः ।

śabdaḥ bandhaḥ ।

Word associations lead to paradox.

Word associations (bindings) lead to paradox because each is true only within the locus of specific time and space. Each perspective shapes the world in its own unique way. When perspectives are compared there are aspects where they don't match.

Words describe the associations of the past, whereas each truly new experience must have something in it that was never described before. Therefore, words are insufficient. Words merely catalogue perceived objects from the point of view of the subject and they cannot describe the subject.

Words bring forth images that bind the individual to the experience, creating an anchor to the past. These words help point to the ultimate basis of experience. Often our only connection with the world is by words from the past.

The past belongs as much to our imagination as do the dreams of the future. The past is fashioned by recounting, and the future is created by imagination.

We are bound to the past by the uniqueness of its shape, created by our interpretive lens; we cannot clearly see the unfolding events of the present. The past must be acknowledged so that one has the words to create a new future.

To command the past is to direct the evolution of the present. The word is bound in multiple ways. According to *R̥V* 10.114.8:

> सहस्रधा पञ्चदशान्युक्था यावद्द्यावापृथिवी तावदित्तत् ।
> सहस्रधा महिमानः सहस्रं यावद्ब्रह्म विष्ठितं तावती वाक् ॥
>
> *sahasradhā pañcadaśanyukthā yāvad dyāvāpr̥thivī tāvadit tat* ।
> *sahasradhā mahimānaḥ sahasraṁ yāvadbrahma viṣṭhitaṁ tāvatī vāk* ॥
>
> Fifteen thousand *uktha mantra*s are ranged as the heavens and earth. Our worship is of a thousand kind, and like it our speech is also boundless.

The image underlying the word is a construct of the mind fashioned out of the objects of the physical world and the abstractions of the inner space of the mind. The image constructed can either lead to apprehension of the universal or become a fetish.

To be bound by names and words for all time is to accept a lesser existence. But this presents a dilemma: can we use words to escape other words?

Names are fundamental to recognition. They imprison; they also provide comfort. Ultimately, names dissolve; they must be transcended.

Mind associates strings of images (scripts) with its activity. These scripts have their grammar, and just like language they create narrative.

Scripts are fashioned by *saṁskāra*s, which are rituals that engage senses and inscribe the mind.

Dreams are scripts strung together as wishes or fears or anticipation of events.

8

भाषा अपरा ।

bhāṣā aparā ।

Linguistic knowledge is of limited kind.

Language is concerned with the finite or at most countably infinite (the *aparā*) projections of reality, which remains greater than the sum of all such projections. In actuality, the projections are finite in ordinary experience.

The process of discretization reduces reality into the world of ordinary associations.

Language can become a vehicle to describe change and transform images. Although limited, it can show the way across different projections. Words lend form to experience.

The flow of experience can occur in countless ways, and each narrative describes one of the infinite stories that exist.

The basis of language is *avidyā*. Says Patañjali:

> अनित्य अशुचि दुःख अनात्मसु ।
> नित्यशुचिसुख आत्मख्यातिः अविद्या ॥
>
> *anitya aśuci duḥkha anātmasu* ।
> *nityaśucisukha ātmakhyātiḥ avidyā* ॥
>
> *Avidyā* is taking the transient, the impure, the painful, and the non-self to be the eternal, the pure, the joyful, and the self. — *Yoga Sūtra*, 2.5

Avidyā is grounded in ego, a consequence of the mistaken identity of the powers of consciousness and the sensory instruments.

As long as a student entertains the thought of his situation, and of his life, he remains in the grip of death and *avidyā*.

To describe is to master. When things are put into narrative they transition from the living and infinite to the dead and finite.

What is expressed by language is secondary. The essential reality is not a symbol, it has no history, it cannot be communicated by words or letters.

Languages are not a creation of logic, but of art, which is why there are so many of them and why they appear to have unique feel.

There are two basic attitudes in art, springing from gender. But since within each one of us exist attitudes, in superior or subordinate mode, related to both genders, a spectrum is formed. Further variety is related to time and emotion.

Art gives intimation of the infinite. Art can shock and awaken, which is its true role. This it does not in itself, but in the meeting of the self with it, by jolting the experiencer out of ordinary state of being.

Behind art rests a paradox, an irrational essence, but its own enlargements and amplifications strive for a consistency at the surface level. As the language enlarges, its expressions may become so rich that its parts may come to be contradictory. The language may then split into daughter languages in seemingly discrete jumps.

Art is endlessly renewing. A poem, a picture, an image or a dance can be conceived in ever new ways. Today's art is tomorrow's cliche.

Art is the collective language of people in society embodying the frustrations of individuals in failing to reach their creative destiny.

Art, like words, throws a covering on reality. While it reveals by its contours, it also hides by its form.

Any current art must be transcended by new art.

9

विरुद्धानि इव अपि दर्शनानि परस्परपूरकानि ।

viruddhāni iva api darśanāni paraspara-pūrakāni ।

Darśanas, although seemingly contradictory, are complementary.

Each linguistic view is a window on reality. A *darśana* is such a view that includes consideration of conscious agents. The *darśanas* represent complementary knowledge. The contradiction between them arises out of the different assumptions at the basis of their formal logical structures. To meditate on these differences is to learn the limitations of each perspective.

Imagining oneself to be within a cube, there exist six enclosing walls, and each of these walls is a window on reality. Just as a cube has six sides, there are six basic *darśanas*, which express the three orthogonal views related to traditional rites (Pūrva Mīmāṁsā), atomic analysis of words (Nyāya), and evolution at the personal and cosmic scale (Sāṁkhya) and their complementary positions related to nature of reality (Vedānta), atomic analysis of matter (Vaiśeṣika), and synthesis of spirit and body (Yoga). There arise an infinity of other *darśanas*, which combine the basic six in a variety of combinations that also account for other subjects and passage of time. A *darśana* is experienced as an association with a specific view of reality. The view gets projected on the screen of the mind in terms of an image — visual or abstract. Analysing the image with the use of language provides more complexity.

Each *darśana* seizes the heart, appearing as the sole truth to the experiencer because of the limitation of the mind to hold more than one thing at a time. The experiencer lives life to validate this truth. This attachment is the essence of desire and it leads to grief. This is another way that *māyā* works.

In the statement, *parokṣa priyā iva hi devāḥ, pratyakṣa dviṣaḥ* (परोक्ष प्रिया इव हि देवाः प्रत्यक्ष द्विषः), the devas love what is mysterious (hidden or paradoxical) and detest what is evident, the *pratyakṣa* refers to the linguistic statements or a surface viewing of a process. True understanding recognizes the limitations of any formal ideology.

The *pratyakṣa* of the inner is covered by the *parokṣa* of the outer. There is a recursion in the very definition of inner and outer.

Without experiencing God, one remains a brute. Cruelty arises out of a shrinking of the self so that one remains one's animal self alone.

Growth is the severing of the cords that bind one down to the *paśu*. When these cords are severed, one is a master.

Education is the opening up of different ways of seeing. Just as songbirds must hear songs in a critical window of development, humans must be exposed to different ways of seeing at the right time in their childhood.

10

आन्तरिकस्थितयः परिसंख्यायोग्याः ।

āntarika-sthitayaḥ parisaṁkhyā-yogyāḥ ।

The inner states are countable.

Mind states are countable and discrete because the mind can only perceive sequentially. The individual mind projects the simultaneity of many happenings to an ordered sequence, that becomes the individual's personal truth. Says Akṣapāda Gotama in the *Nyāya- Sūtras* (3.2.56): *jñānāyaugapadyāt ekaṁ manaḥ* (ज्ञानायौगपद्यात् एकं मनः), the mind is one on account of the non-simultaneity of cognition.

Each cognition is illuminated by an inner light, a *deva*. The body is the temple of the *deva*s with the inner fire of the mind holding up the inner sky. The contours of this inner space are made clear by the smoke trailing this fire.

Because of the *bandhu*s, the inner devas are mirrored in the leaders of society. A multitude of *deva*s guarantees a government of many.

A tradition that accepts only a single god is not an appropriate environment for the rule of the many. A jealous god begets jealous individuals.

Corresponding to the mind states are specific centres in the brain. It is this discreteness that is reflected in some patients of brain trauma or stroke in phenomena such as alexia without agraphia, which is the ability to write without the corresponding ability to read.

It is possible for a person to have acute ability of one kind or another without a general development of wisdom or intelligence.

Animals are better than humans at certain things. Their inner states are like our own, but they lack *vijñāna*. Machines can do even better than animals, but here we are certain that they do not possess awareness.

The discrete states serve as the ground on which the *deva*s emerge.

The *deva*s are interdependent. Their power is not accessible to those who don't recognize them.

Consciousness is present as the Witness, but it is manifest in its recognizable form only in living beings. Ordinary consciousness is contingent on specific brain states.

When there is damage to the brain, the nature of the experience changes. When the senses are not in harmony, the world likewise gets distorted, leading to delusion.

11

भाषालोकविरुद्धाभासातीतं विज्ञानम् ।

bhāṣā-loka-viruddha-ābhāsa-atītaṁ vijñānaṁ ।

Vijñāna *is beyond language and paradox.*

Ordinary knowledge is accompanied by doubt. True knowledge (*parā*) is beyond paradox: it is universal and *pratyakṣa*. At the deepest layer, there is no duality. *Parokṣa* is the covering of art on the canvas of *pratyakṣa*. The words of *parokṣa* conceal the vision of *pratyakṣa*.

True knowledge can only be experienced and not described because words, by definition, set up a separation between subject and object. Truth is in the experience.

How to distinguish true knowledge from delusion? An assertion is not enough because how is one to distinguish it from pretense or a desire to impress or false knowledge? Even conviction in one's experience does not suffice.

True experience comes with many signs, such as compassion (*karuṇā*) and friendship (*maitrī*). It leads to an expansion of the self in an embrace that includes other beings. It comes with wisdom and understanding and it may be inferred with questioning.

It also leads to uncommon knowledge, such as insight that may not be available from an inquiry using ordinary science.

The individual has multiple selves within. Two of these are the body and the inner controller, but the body itself has many multiplicities arising springing from time, past visions, and desire. Delusion — and mental suffering — arises out of unreconciled multiplicity within. Suffering is made worse by imitating those whom we cannot resemble.

Vijñāna leads to a soaring of the spirit, providing new perspectives.

Going up seems the most natural process until one sees the world sink underneath and find much of art and music to be repetition.

12

यज्ञात् प्रज्ञा आविर्भवति ।

yajñāt prajñā āvirbhavati ।

Prajñā emerges out of *yajña*.

Understanding emerges out of the self-transformation of *yajña*; understanding is in itself a state of mind. Mind affects matter just as matter affects mind.

Yajña requires ethical discipline (*dharma*) because if there were fractured selves within, the stress due to the unequal evolution of each of these selves will bring suffering and pain.

Ultimately, the mind must pull itself up, by its bootstraps as it were, from the bog of surface associations. The success of *yajña* is contingent on a transcendent leap. The change is like a pull by a higher, subtle force.

Yajña is also a change from earlier state, a sacrifice of what one is, to become new. It is a moment of creation.

The obverse side of creation is death. The success of *yajña* depends on confronting death. It is the recognition of ordinary mortality that makes each moment alive.

Transformation is obtained by ritual that engages the senses and compels a journey beyond ordinary boundaries, by expanding the self in society, and enlarging it into divinity.

Transformation is not by going with the surface flow of events, but by restraint.

Transformation is achieved through love, especially that which is unselfish and universally given. Somewhat like dying, loving requires that one erase one's ordinary self, making it possible to see things in new ways as one has ceased to be what one was before.

Detachment and love, aloneness and mingling are two ends that help find reach the middle ground of wisdom. Detachment by itself is not enough; neither is reckless love.

Detachment that strengthens love towards everyone leads to transformation.

Yajña proceeds in the world on a continuing basis. *Yajña* is an ongoing struggle between the word and image. It is joy to be harnessed to a greater *yajña*.

Life is a game to learn the laws of self. One knows the end but the journey provides delight.

For the youth, *yajña* is an experience that becomes a doorway; for the old, it is merely a passage.

Ethical discipline sets forth a chain of change. According to Jaimini: *codanālakṣaṇo 'rtho dharmaḥ* (चोदनालक्षणोऽर्थो धर्मः), dharma is that which is conducive to the highest good (*Mīmāṁsā-Sūtra*s 1.1.2).

13

चित्तमाव्रियते वर्णैः ।

cittam-āvriyate varṇaiḥ ।

Colours (of changing hue) are the coverings of the mind.

Mind may assume different states like that of the analyser, the doer, the aesthete, and the sustainer. Each mind is associated with all these states in random succession. Brāhmaṇa, rājanya, vaiśya, and śūdra are states that characterize each individual, as do the devas. There exist āsuric and *paśu* states as well.

The *varṇa* states arise from different proportions of *sattva*, *rajas*, and *tamas*. These proportions do not remain constant in an individual, but change in different ways depending on time, place and circumstance. Each human, being in the image of *puruṣa*, has tendencies that mirror the processes of growth, preservation and destruction, changing according to the environment. Education makes steady those states that are harmonious.

We are born with potential that is our biological inheritance. But the actual flowering of our selves depends on the life experience. Education and discipline are essential for a transformation of colours (*varṇa*).

Transformation may be achieved by training of body, breath, mind, imagination, and by compassion. Since the mind states are held steady in the body states, the latter play an important role. It is sometimes easier to fix the inner state by training the body.

Even when steady in a single state, it is essential to range across other colours to provide a steadying background.

The process may be started by emphasizing any one of these that address the different sheaths of the self. The man of knowledge teaches and guides the man in ignorance.

Pain is felt when the process of change does not flow harmoniously. As Gotama says: *bādhanālakṣaṇaṁ duḥkham iti* (बाधनालक्षणं दुःखम् इति), pain is the characteristic of the restraint [of the self] (*Nyāya-Sūtras* 1.1.21).

The pain of the body makes people oblivious to what lies beyond it. When the capacity to experience grief is lost, fiction is the only solace.

Any idea, no matter how desirable in itself, becomes a prison if the mind is obsessed with it. This is true even of the desire for freedom and knowledge. These are merely the outcomes of finding the space that provides harmony with the universe.

14

पशुअसुरराक्षस आत्मनि निवसन्ति ।

paśu-asura-rākṣasa ātmani nivasanti ।

Animals, *asuras*, and *rākṣasas* reside within.

The inner states include those of animal, the materialist (*asura*), and the possessor (*rākṣasa*). Each person has the tendency to acquire and command, create and destroy.

There are two kinds of people. First, those who see themselves in relationship of power: they must either dominate the weak or submit before the powerful. Second, those who believe they are neither superior nor inferior to others, accepting that everyone is fired by the same transcendent spirit. The first kind tread the āsuric path, the second the path of the warrior.

The first is the path of darkness, the second the path of light. The first is the path of stasis, the second the path of continuing change and struggle.

The dark way holds the mind in bondage. The path of freedom is the path of the strong. The warrior must be prepared for all exigencies.

Since evolution and change is the natural condition of nature, there is an unceasing struggle between individuals and cultures that represent different paths. The forces of light and dark recruit those with energy to their side in this contest.

By bringing about rapid evolution in material and cultural conditions, science has unleashed long dormant forces of light and dark in society, as also in individuals. Due to this the next few years will witness serious conflict between the forces of light and dark.

Such a battle cannot be wished away. But its intensity could be checked by the spread of knowledge. The mission of spreading outer and inner science must be embraced by awakened people to show the path of light to the larger public.

The future will bring growth and development as nature passes through another cycle of transformation.

15

पशुत्वस्य नाशनम् एव मुक्तिः ।

paśutvasya nāśanam eva muktiḥ ।

Mukti is the vanquishing of the [inner] animal selves.

Freedom from reflexive behaviour is obtained by transcending one's animal selves. In truth, one must also transcend other selves, but some of them are essential for cognition. Reflexive behaviour is animal behaviour.

Yajña is inspired behaviour that changes the inner states to one of greater harmony.

To be free is to have the privilege to peep into the process of change and contribute to its happening. To be free is to be in, or part of, *sat*. To be free is to have become a god.

This freedom has a certainty, somewhat like that of reflexivity, but, in truth, it is entirely different.

I am free when I think I am not, and not free when I think I am.

To recognize is to vanquish. Self-recognition is a way to power.

The way of the warrior is the way of extreme discipline, of being fully aware. The warrior lives as if this day is the last, since one doesn't know what is to come tomorrow.

Mukti is the disappearance of the mind and becoming one with the action, as was true of Arjuna with his bow when he shot the moving fish by looking at its reflection in the pan of oil.

If life is using the sword of discrimination in fighting *saṁsāra* for *nirvāṇa,* the mind should be transferred to the sword itself. If it were to be concentrated on any particular place in the body, the enemy would strike at that point.

Although the mind may be one-pointed at a certain place, it should be allowed to suffuse the entire body.

The mind is ordinarily intellectually or rationally burdened. It cannot move from one thing to another without stopping or reflecting on itself. When the mind is self-conscious, it ceases to flow by itself and it becomes hesitant, calculating, and deliberative.

A mind unconscious of itself is not disturbed by irrelevant things. It is in a state of no-mind, without obstructions, with promise of freedom. Paradoxically, the mind is most powerful when it is in the state of no-thinking.

One cannot sit still, because doing that would mean that one has accepted a fixed state, torpor or death. In the words of *Aitareya Brāhmaṇa* 7.14:

कलिः शयनो भवति
संजिहानस्तु द्वापरः
उत्तिष्ठंस्त्रेता भवति
कृतंसम्पद्यते चरंश्च
चरैवेति। चरैवेति।

kaliḥ śayano bhavati
saṁjihānastu dvāparaḥ
uttiṣṭhaṁstretā bhavati
kṛtaṁsampadyate caraṁś
caraiveti, caraiveti ।

He is [in] *Kali* when he lays down,
Dvāpara when he rises,
Tretā when he stands erect,
And [in] *Kṛta* when he moves.
Therefore, move on, move on!

चरन्वै मधु विन्दति
चरन्स्वादुमुदुमम्बरम्
सूर्यस्य पश्य श्रेमाणं
यो न तन्द्रयते चरंश
चरैवेति। चरैवेति।

caranvai madhu vindati
caransvādumudumbaram
sūryasya paśya śremāṇaṁ
yo na tandrayate caraṁś
caraiveti, caraiveti ।

Moving one finds honey,
Moving the sweet *udumbara* [fruit],
See the lordship of the sun,
who tires not of its motions.
Therefore, move on, move on!

The victory of the self requires victory over the *paśu* nature. It requires constant vigilance.

16

यज्ञो योगः परिणामः परिवर्तनं च ।

yajño yogaḥ pariṇāmaḥ parivartanaṁ ca ।

Yajña is yoga, which is becoming and transformation.

The process of self-transformation is the conjunction (*yoga*) of the opposites within. For each of the opposites, there is a different kind of *yoga*. Ethical discipline (*dharma*) makes these come together, making transcendence possible. This requires *śraddhā* (faith) and *anugraha* (grace).

It is like swimming. Without having tried it, or without having seen someone do it, one might consider it impossible. Likewise, without seeing birds fly, man may have never thought of creating machines that are also able to do so.

Yoga brings together opposites within, making it possible to go beyond them. *Yoga* is at the meeting point of previously established states. It generates new balance, creating new possibilities.

In *yoga* there is no *varṇa*, no self, no limitation, and one experiences a freedom from *saṁskāras*. Patañjali says that in *yoga* –– *tadā draṣṭuḥ svarūpe 'vasthānaṁ* (तदा द्रष्टुः स्वरूपेऽवस्थानं) (*Yoga-Sūtras* 1.3), the seer is established in his own nature. When one lapses out of *yoga*, the usual tendencies reassert themselves, one becomes one's ordinary social self.

Out of *yoga*, one puts on one's social mask. Expectations related to one's social role drive behaviour.

One's own self is hidden from oneself. Our opinion of ourselves varies more often than our opinion of others.

Recognition of the self is facilitated by seeing one's reflection in other individuals. Its clarity depends on the transparency of the other person. This recognition comes as an awareness of its different aspects.

Yajña is the doorway to understanding the mystery of time. It takes one to the essential experience of *yoga*. Different *yajña*s are needed for the different kinds of *yoga*. They need not be according to custom. New forms remain to be discovered that will serve in facilitating the passage to the new state.

17

शरीरमनसि असम्भूतिसम्भूति अविद्याविद्ये पक्षाविव ।

śarīra-manasi asambhūti-sambhūti avidyā-vidye pakṣāviva ।

Body and mind, materiality and life, rules and understanding are like wings.

Mind cannot be by itself. Body and mind are like two wings that balance each other. Each builds upon the strivings of the other.

Between subject and object there is a gap. We see ourselves located at the gap, or stretched across both at the same time. We feel in one and name in the other.

There is a fundamental vibration (*spandan*) in which the two wings are seen one after the other. The world appears as wholly body, and then as wholly mind.

Light requires the background of darkness. Like day and night, the *deva*s and *asura*s are complementary.

The opposites must be recognized and used creatively for transformation. The recognition requires that one learns to be in harmony with the inner nature.

Bring the opposites together in a state of amity and compassion. By harnessing the *asura* to the vision of the *deva, sat* is realized effortlessly.

Yoga builds an inner ladder to climb in the inner sky. This ladder becomes useless, or unnecessary, when one has reached above the brush and it is possible to take off. One also needs to make room out of the clutter to run so as to pick up speed to begin the flight.

Learning to flap the wings in unison requires effort and practice. Just climbing on it for higher ground does not guarantee success.

The flapping of the wings requires learning to transition from one state to its opposite, and back again, in a relentless dance. This *spandan* is not across just two states, but many opposites. After effort, the *spandan*, the transition, holds steady, and this steadiness becomes the dominant mode of being, superseding more basic states.

But even before one can take-off, possibilities become evident. One begins to dream, and see the vision of what is to come.

18

प्रज्ञा ऐश्वर्यं पक्षिणः उड्डयनम्।

prajñā aiśvaryaṁ pakṣiṇaḥ uḍḍayanam ।

Prajñā is *aiśvarya* — the soaring of the [inner] bird.

True understanding is a state like a bird in flight. It is a movement, a process, that cannot be frozen into a fixed shape.

For reality to become experienceable, it is essential that the one unfold into two, and these two become the ground on which further unfoldment through time may occur. The two wings represent the two sides that enable this movement.

At the experiential level, one must not believe that one is bound to the earth. To fly is to be in ceaseless motion, so that motion itself, the true unfolding of self, becomes the primary experience. A masterful flight is a thing of beauty and joy. It is a whole that cannot be broken into parts. The flight is the journey and it is the goal.

There is no ownership in flight, only companionship; there is no domination, only a bond that reaches across everyone in the flock, with the stragglers influencing the leaders and the other way round.

The play of consciousness is a play for the edification of the senses, of the *deva*s. A flight across unending desert or unending waters will be sterile. If the outer world is free, it becomes possible to see the pervading beauty of the inner world match that of the outer.

Mountains and streams, valleys and rolling deserts, forests and fruit trees of the inner can then match those of the outer. It is the measure of the one against the other that make it possible to recognize.

If the outer is controlled by machines and made into an artifical garden, it would become impossible to relate to the beauty of the inner, causing an alienation that becomes the way of death.

As the world becomes more organized and controlled by machines, the sense of alienation and despair will increase. The empire controlled by machines will be challenged by warriors fighting to restore freedom and creativity. This would be a struggle between *asura*s and *deva*s on a global scale. Although this fight is as old as history it is now being fought with weapons stronger than ever before.

The *vīra rasa* of the warrior transforms into the passion of *śṛṅgāra*. The contemplation of the battle is untroubled by desire or evil. One is not slave to the will.

But the *vīra* or *śṛṅgāra rasa* is only a passing covering (*āvaraṇa*). Thoughts of others make one distressed on account of their suffering. One may also become one with every other being, as an expression of the universal will. Compassion alternates with an overpowering renunciation, a desire to nullify will itself. Compassion and renunciation are the two wings of the flight.

Individual destiny is not unique and separate from that of other beings. One's flight is part of the larger movement of other beings.

Understanding is rooted in the reality of the lived world as an expression of truth.

True understanding brings with it an ability to see beauty. The world appears as an interconnected whole. It is a thing of delight.

4

The Self and Recursion

WE now consider implications of these *sūtras* to our understanding of self. Although there is a unity underlying reality, one's ordinary experience can only be in terms of dualities. Commonsensical understanding is based on associations and logical inference and, therefore, it must be reductionist. But common sense cannot deal with questions of self, which emerge the moment one makes an attempt to define the experiencer, the "I" who is making inferences.

Limitations of Language

Between the outer reality and the experiencing self lies the agency of the mind. This middle space can only be addressed by metaphysics — where words stretch to provide insight that cannot be reduced to simple declarations.

Although metaphysics deals with existence and reality, its formal study is limited to narratives on reality and existence, and their linguistic analysis. The study of knowledge and ethics is also mutually dependent and related to politics and aesthetics, which are choices in the field of force and power and the sense of art and life. But due to the limitations of language, these conceptions are shadows whose original form remains elusive.

Language is limited because it can only relate to relations between things, whereas reality concerns change, and things are continually transformed. Language expresses associations between things in a sequential manner, whereas their unfolding is simultaneous and parallel. Nevertheless, language provides the structure with which we construct our ordinary view of reality and although this view is limited, analysis of meaning can help obtain important and deeper insight. In particular, such analysis makes one aware of paradoxes that inform us of the limitations of our knowledge.

The beginning cannot be unitary, because the one cannot, by itself, become many. The one must be defined in relation to others. There can neither be only one, nor many at the beginning, because that would undermine order, and imply perennial chaos. The beginning must thus not be of things, but of the order itself, together with the potential for all its manifestations.

When manifestations reside as impressions they become the ground on which further expressions of the recursion takes place.

Recursion is logical. When viewed in the mind's eye, one becomes aware of duality out of which mathematics is born.

Brain and mind are not identical. The self is the bridge that spans the many layers of being. But the brain is the base on which the mind rests, therefore its examination can reveal the higher layers of being by pointing to the paradox in assuming otherwise. The interrelationships in the outside world, in the physical world as well as in society, are mirrored in the organization of the brain.

Metaphysics cannot be reduced to logic: it deals with paradox and inversion. Art and creative action illustrates this most clearly. Time flies into the future, but we live facing the past, burdened by it. What we seek in search of happiness is precisely what is sure to bring despair. Although we speak of the world as a collection of things, we can only celebrate impermanence. This impermanence has a recursionist foundation, expressed in repetitive patterns.

Mind's Evolution

Reality is process and representations. Process itself is seen in the mind as motion of objects, which are defined in terms of location in time and space in change. Since representations are sequential, reality is seen in slices that are put together by the mind.

A causal change underlies objects in change. There is a logical basis to representation, and action follows intention. When assembling the slices together, the mind imposes a larger logic on them.

The object has several forms associated with it. First is the physical form in transformation; second is its rational or logical form; and third is its causal form. The object also has a unique emotional content.

Mind in motion is an object with the representations of the outer and the inner worlds as its fields. Reasoning emerges out of the capacity to make abstract representations.

Mind's evolution depends on representations, innate nature, and intention. Since representations and innate nature are an expression of the past and being, the world, as understood by mind, is created by it.

Intentions cannot belong to the world of objects because they would then be subject to causality and thus not be free. They must transcend space and time, and be a part of the order underlying recursion.

The process of evolution is accompanied by expansion and enlargement, growth and decay. This is true both at the individual and social levels. It is also true of mental objects.

The Power of Impressions

Impressions assume iconic power after they have been embellished in the theatre of the mind. They become the scaffolding for the construction of personal reality in which things are glued together by hopes and dreams. This is a reality that can come crashing down if it runs into conflict with other actualities. The interplay of these realities has a logic that becomes apparent when one moves beyond appearances to relationships and patterns of change.

Recursion is an expression of the fundamental laws of nature. It is more than structural relationship, for it is to be seen both at the physical and the abstract levels as also across relational entities. Recursionism provides a way of knowing as it helps us find meaning by a shift in perspective and by abstraction. It is the unitary unifying principle in Nature.

As we learn to recognize the same forces and patterns recurring on different levels, we are able to unite these levels and their diverse phenomena into a meaningful and organic whole. But the manner in which this structure is put together represents a larger meaning, which is a consequence of the underlying aesthetics.

Recursionism refers not only to replicated form but also to nesting across scale and time. It emerges out of the same elements combining repeatedly at different levels. It encompasses form and function. Mind is the embodiment of the infinite regress of this recursion. Without such regress mind cannot emerge, and since machines cannot be designed to have recursive structure, they will never be conscious.

Objective reality is bound by logic and relationships. The recursive order behind it does not lie in space and time; it is transcendent.

Beauty, which is recursive symmetry, and power, which is recursive asymmetry, both appeal across form. Evolution is a dance of beauty and power, where broken symmetries become the basis for new symmetry. The dance of the peacock attracts not only the peahen but also the human. Animal displays have universal significance.

At the deepest level, there is no meaning; only symmetries or pure play.

Power and expansion is basic to evolution. It is repeated from the smallest structures to the largest ones. Social structures also reflect dominance and growth; therefore, they are also subject to decay and extinction.

Art is the creation of archetypal patterns. Since the structure of natural patterns is concealed by the chaos of the surface forms, good art mimics concealment and recursion. In performance, poetry, and narrative, meaning is best communicated by suggestion. A word, with its suggestive power, is worth a thousand pictures.

The experience of the creative expression makes one aware of its source within oneself. Art is the best education for self-development.

The nature of cognitive systems is determined by the underlying biology. Therefore, biological forms are fundamental to art and social organization. But just as there are innumerable biological forms, made even more numerous by growth and decay, there are innumerable cognitive systems.

Each cognitive window comes with its own recursive logic. Natural, logical, creative or artificial languages express unique perspective. Recursion turns this perspective into a signature that is seen across other cognitive tasks.

Patterns repeat within biological structures, and they are replicated in artificial forms such as dresses, toys, machines, monuments, and in art and architecture. The forms that Nature makes are the models for our own creations. Forms at one scale mimic those at the other. Patterns also repeat in the use of artificial signs.

Ideas are like organisms. They replicate and die like biological entities. They have similar relationships, and also a generative unity. The web of ideas is similar to the web of life. Ideas also have their ambiguities because of the ambiguities in the models of things that concretize them in our minds.

Recursionism across species implies that our behavioural patterns are determined by biology just like for animals.

Freedom is the urge to perform by instinct; it is the urge to find harmony. Those who think they are free are not;

those who appear to be in harmony with the world around them are.

Language — both in the inner and social discourse — opens up new worlds of possibilities, spawning whole universes within. This brings opposites together creating a unique tension. Words express the recurrent essence of phenomena. Meaning is only possible because of recurrence.

Animals have the same spectrum of emotions that humans possess. It is through the lens of emotion that we communicate with animals. Feeling is higher than thinking. Cognitive categories come in wholes!

Each organism makes sense of the world within its field of activity. Our pet, an Australian cockatiel, has lived with us for over eleven years. One would think that living in a totally alien environment would confuse the bird, but he has special relationship with different members of the family, and unique ritual related to play and ownership. Bird and man understand each other at various emotional levels because of the common recursively expressed structure.

The ability to communicate with each other amongst humans, just like that of other animals, is a consequence of recursionism, which defines a common ground on which experience of different people is like a relief.

Recursionism is the explanation why in an ant colony the castes adjust their populations to maintain definite proportion; it is the explanation of why new biological forms emerge in the evolutionary chain.

Recursionism reflects a universal imperative towards greater unfoldment of existing structures. It is a self-organizing, self-regulating principle which allows for growth as well.

Continuing conflict in society mirrors the interplay of oppositions in physical and biological worlds. There is reason in our animal self and madness in our human self. We seek reason in search for destiny that we absolutely abhor.

As animals, humans live their lives according to some specific script, derived from one of many religious or social ideologies. Each ideology is a frozen view, limiting freedom. The tail of the emotional dog is perfectly rational; the animals of the wild act according to their nature. Our being has automaticity at as many levels as we can think.

Freedom is the capacity to choose one of the ideologies, although one becomes a prisoner as soon as one has made the choice. Creativity is the capacity to jump across the ideologies to connect to the archetypal patterns of existence and appearance.

Recursionism is also at work across space, time, function, and form for processes of generation and transition. Evolution is a manifestation of recursion in increasing complexity.

The process of recursion works across many levels, creating multitude of appearances at the level of the individual minds and in their many narratives.

Unity exists on different levels of manifestation. Order becomes apparent in the background of chaos when we identify the appropriate scale on which the phenomenon is projected.

Globalization is a recursionist process that is transforming the world system into an organism with components that have extreme specialization. The war against the other, that characterized colonial expansion, will be replaced by war against previous selves. Rather than war to capture physical space and property, the new war will be to dominate history.

5

Languages of the Brain

REFLECTING on moments past, one is often surprised at one's thoughts and actions, even if the circumstances in which they occurred were different. In justifications of one's own history to oneself, it is common to ascribe those thoughts and actions to the severity of the situation, in acceptance of the view that we are not free agents and merely respond to forces around us.

On the other hand, we know that often our suffering is generated by the play within our inner world, and mental pain can be as severe as physical pain. If one has thought of ending one's life in response to inner suffering, then it is clear that there is at least one self within who, at the time of that dark thought, did not consider life worth living. But this is inherently paradoxical, because why should the self, if it is emergent on the body, wish for the body to cease to be; and if it is independent of the body, feel despair at the condition of the person and his history?

It seems that one is not a single self, although there is some common thread holding these disparate incarnations. This commonality is more than our personal history; it is the "self" with its unique attitude, "the inner being" at its core, who is distinct from others. At other times it appears that there are several selves within, which interpose almost simultaneously in such a disjointed manner that one feels that there may be processes in our brain that are quite outside of one's control.

Constructing Reality

I was motivated to gather together my thoughts on these questions over ten years ago in response to a request to write a chapter on my philosophical ideas on brain function in a neuroscience book. In this chapter, I wrote about a hierarchy of brain functions, arguing that first of all the brain has a holistic character, reflected in processes that are related to the conscious and the unconscious selves; second, it changes its very organization by adjusting to its sensory environment as if it has the capacity to understand what is happening outside; and, finally, it has other processes that are associative, which are amenable to straightforward mathematical and logical analysis.

I showed that there were other processes in nature that have similar modes of expression, and this was suggestive that they existed in the brain. I summarized the physiological evidence in favour of these three languages. In particular, I spoke about how the very models we construct of reality are mediated by the mind.

I classified brain behaviour into three modes and not more because these three are qualitatively different categories. The quantum considers the system as one whole, and inherent in that is the potential for the variety of its evolutionary paths; the reorganization implies a blind agency within the components of the system that lies beyond the reductionist paradigm; and the associative is in accord with reductionism.

The logics that are involved in each are different: superpositional in the case of quantum, active and goal-seeking in the case of reorganizational, and classical, machine-like in the case of associative. It is obvious that to assume that they unfold serially is only a simplifying assumption. In reality, the three logics are at play simultaneously, and if ordinary science considers mainly the classical, it captures only one aspect of reality. The three are untangled by the agency of the subject, and to this extent understanding is an artefact of the consciousness of the subject.

The three logics are the bases of our three lives. It is of course quite possible to see further divisions in each of these modes. In particular, the term "quantum" in the context of personal experience could mean different things to different people — the holistic experience could relate to the spirit or the body.

I didn't get a chance in my brain essay to speak of how modes of human and social expression parallel the languages of the brain. These parallels are of greater interest to the layperson than the technical problem of brain behaviour. These other languages manifest themselves in different kinds of speech, and also in social and economic organization.

Language Related to Tradition, Rules, and Ritual

It provides satisfaction and security and connection to past and one's community. This represents the most basic animal part of our being. Most of the rules relate to social expression, although some others may relate to abstract entities. Principally, this language concerns the world of things, sensations, experience, ownership and power. It is also a part of religious ritual and secular ceremony. Its more intricate forms are seen in dance and music and that experience is heightened by recognition of these patterns.

Language Related to Change and Adjustment

In contrast to the previous language, it concerns innovation to the ritual with time. It includes within its ambit more than one's personal self, and it may, in its more evolved form, include other animals, and indeed all life. This language is ecological in that it seeks rationalization of one's place in the world by bringing in larger purpose, which is greater than that of one's own personal gain. This language provides the capacity to go beyond possession and consider the family, the community, and race, humanity, and all life.

Language Related to Transcendent Experience

This emerges out of the desire to go beyond ritual and descriptions in terms of finite space and time. This transcendence could be either related to the body or the spirit or a combination of both. Some see it in love or sexuality, while others see it as a mystical, spiritual experience. It is the experience of the artist, the scientist, and the philosopher, and the epiphany at the sight of a sunrise or sunset. It is also the happiness found in friendship, love, or sacrifice. By its very nature it cannot be part of the normal linguistic discourse, therefore, this communication is by means of hints, allusion and suggestion, by poetry and art.

These three modes of expression — let's call them Language *A*, *B*, and *C*, respectively — are connected together by entities that straddle the boundaries between them. Language *A* is associated with power and pleasure, and in its limits it reveals paradox; Language *B* is associated with connections and concern, and it gives rise to compassion; and Language *C* is associated with insight and awareness, and it leads to wisdom.

We see the three languages at work in stage during the different phases of a child's education. Whereas words are sufficient to describe Languages *A* and *B*, the nature of Language *C* is ambiguous and it is not easy to communicate its experience directly.

From another perspective, Language *A* concerns ritual, Language *B* is about evolution, and Language *C* is about self-awareness. For those who have been taught that the world is about tradition, it is inconceivable that evolution could be true. For those who have learnt to see evolution as a function emergent on material ground, it is inconceivable that their awareness could be anything more than an epiphenomenon.

Ritual and Meaning

Rules and ritual, whether related to social behaviour, bureaucratic structures, law, or organized religion, provide comfort. But often they become the end rather than the means to the exploration of the spirit, thus creating profound alienation and emptiness. Having learnt these rules, one wishes to change them, and to go beyond them to change oneself — become a "better person" — do something for community, for country, for mankind, and for all of nature by being its steward. But this change comes with the fear of impending loss, of recognition that it all is a mere twinkling of an eye of something that will all end before long.

It brings the insight that anything finite and bound by rules could not be the explanation of the mystery of one's own being, and it awakens a yearning for a sense that is beyond pain and suffering. But in order to reach this experience one is prepared to abandon all, go beyond the worlds of the first two languages, and put up with any suffering and pain. So powerful is the promise of the infinite, the breath of the eternal!

These languages have several layers within them. Language *A*, for example, can address rules at different levels. Even when one is operating within its domain, one can go from the state of submission to that of power. Each has rules, but the nature of the rules and the degree of control may be different. This explains how a system that is fundamentally oppressive would be embraced by someone who thinks that it opens the doors to a mode of behaviour which is like that of a tiger, when earlier the person had lived like a sheep. Since the systems of rules have much variety, one can find immense aesthetic pleasure in living life through the prism of Language *A*. This constitutes life in most societies, where there are very few individuals openly challenging the rules, seeking a revolution, or speaking of the misery of life that is completely ordered.

Language *B* communicates combinatorial insight and it provides new ways of looking at tradition and the creation of new tradition and style. It is, therefore, associated with normal creativity and leadership in business, religion, and politics.

Language *C*, perhaps the anti-language, is about the experiencing self, the subject. It is most elusive. It is mostly remembered in terms of the changes that it brings about in the self, in one's character. This may be viewed as the discourse of the spirit, and the language behind true creativity. But others take it to imply sensuality alone, and this identification can have significant implications for a society.

All vital cultures have elements of the three languages in them, making it possible to live creative lives for those who seek it. Most organized religions are primarily about rules and the perpetuation of the power of its bureaucracy and priesthood. Some religious traditions have evolved so that limited reinterpretation is permitted, so as to remain consistent with self-evident truths. Only few religious traditions emphasize spiritual quest. Most religions are retrogressive and project racial or ethnic pride.

Growth and Change

Just as Languages *B* and *C* emerge out of Language *A*, there is a similar emergence within the individual's development and a society's history. Therefore, a culture or political system that forces absolute obedience to its rules does not have room in it for people to grow beyond the oppressive Language *A*. Such a culture would not support creativity, and one measure of the vitality of the culture is a continuing stream of creative work.

It is imperative that education be devised to facilitate the natural development of the three languages within the individual's life. Education cannot just be about teaching of rules and systems, but also of the freedom and creativity that makes it possible to go beyond existing rules and systems.

In the age of globalization, and of powerful world-ranging machines and organizations, the potential for oppression by bureaucracies, whether of society or state, is greater than ever before. This ought to have been the age of science and liberty, but the rejection of freedom is turning this for many people into an age of fanatic certitude.

Faith becomes the prison that institutions of organized religion employ to keep people bound to them. But even in such a circumstance, people preserve their autonomy by devising their personal interpretations of the official religious myth, which is more in accord with natural law.

Selfhood and Pain

The potential for suffering is inherent in the scheme of the languages. Perhaps the real source of this suffering is the awareness that there is a fundamental lie at the basis of the rules, which suggest a permanence that simply does not exist. Language *A* concerns things, real or abstract, and since things can only be acquired and possessed, acquisition is a primary consequence of this perspective on reality. Since things decay, man has created higher entities that are taken to be permanent. These entities are associated with measure which mitigates the relentless count of days. A count of victories and money and statistics seem, in the rules of Language *A*, to negate the power of time.

Language *B* shows that the definition of entities itself is a result of evolution and past histories of the component systems, denying uniqueness to identity, which is cause of pain. Language *C* peels away individual history, and although this should bring in even more pain and despair, subjects claim that it leads to calm and a strange understanding. By so doing, it preserves its counterintuitive, non-rational nature.

For those who don't have access to the intuitions of Language *C*, the rationality of Languages *A* and *B* is all that can be used to find meaning. Stories about athletes, actors, politicians, business people, writers, wealth, power and investments provide the context in which the individual can measure his or her own march in time. What makes life bearable is an inner count that mitigates the fearfulness of the outer count. But there are also deliberate transgressions of law in the secret sphere of each individual's life. It is as if surviving such transgressions implies transcendence and a victory over fate.

Such transgressions are the modern analog of the ritual sacrifice of the ancient religion. But whereas the ancient performance was out in the open, with participation by everyone, the modern performance is furtive and haphazard. Religious ritual has been replaced by coming-of-age drug parties and promiscuous sex.

6

The Fourth Way

MATERIALISM, prophetic religion, and rational spirituality are three common approaches to perplexing questions about life. They provide their own answers to who we are and what our life means. Since ideas are the means to power, the followers of these approaches are often in violent conflict with each other. People may see events through a blurry theological lens, yet in states of heightened passion small differences can turn to anger and war.

Each of these approaches is fundamentally antithetical to self rule by the people. Materialism is most consonant with the rule of the wealthy elite; prophetic religion to the rule of the clergy or their surrogates; and rational spirituality to the rule of the intellectual elite.

There can be no basis for true democracy until one trusts not only oneself to have access to knowledge but also all others. This requires faith that each person has infinite potential and he does not need an intermediary to apprehend it, something that neither of the above three approaches acknowledges.

Body, Sensations, and Power

Materialism considers mind as an emergent phenomenon that is subsidiary to the body. Ownership of things and sense gratification are two central drives within this paradigm. This view provides great energy to people to work hard to obtain wealth, yet it also leads to alienation and emptiness, and we see this in destructive behaviour, and a culture of drugs, greed, cruelty, and selfishness.

Materialism is the mainstream view of science, but it is unable to explain many scientific problems. In particular, it cannot reconcile the freedom of the individual to its own program of causal order. Neither can it explain how awareness arises in the brain machine when it is absent in the computer machine. It cannot explain the reality of the self in the individual.

The classical materialistic position, as contained in pre-modern physics, was superseded by the advent of relativity theory and quantum mechanics. In particular, quantum theory makes a distinction between the process and the observer, and the privileged position of the observer appears to be irreconcilable to the idea of the primacy of matter.

Mind is relegated to a secondary position, but this makes it seek attention in different ways. Modern medicine responds to these cries of the mind by drugs that often harm the person. There is an estimate that 40 to 50 per cent of people in the rich countries are on psychiatric drugs that sedate them and prevent them from being in touch with their own selves.

Life in the materialistic, machine paradigm values combinatorial intelligence. Science and scholarship are the search for associations to reveal patterns in the physical world, including that of the body. But such associations can never capture the self.

It is not that the materialist does not acknowledge the spirit; only that it is made secondary. The spirit is taken for granted, and words like values, tradition, professional or national cause are employed to ensure that the individual works hard and faithfully for the success of the larger societal machine of which he is a cog.

Without self-knowledge, individuals do not know how to emerge successfully out of the maze of emotions. The template of the jigsaw puzzle, taught to them at school and home, is not a deep enough lesson to experience true transformation and change in their lives.

Materialism was the great impetus for colonization and conquest. For a long time, this was the colonization of unknown countries and subjugation of alien cultures. Now that such colonization is complete, man has entered the phase of colonization of body and mind, which is being done by drug companies, colleges and universities, and the entertainment and information media.

The stars of the materialistic approach are celebrities and entertainers. At work in the machine system, a person must conform to their rhythms; at home, one witnesses disrobing of the performers. Since human contact at workplace has become minimized, one lives on ersatz emotion and in virtual reality.

Visions and Prophecy

It might sound logical to say that we are just our bodies, but, deep within, the individual is certain that this view does not capture all. This is why people pay heed when someone comes along and speaks of visions.

Although the individual is a part of a controlled world, there is the desire within to subvert this constructed reality: hence submission to far-fetched notions, and acceptance of impossible stories.

Prophetic religion demands a suspension of logic. Based on myth and promise, it appeals to the fundamental human urge to control and conquer. Since there are several prophetic religions, each claiming to be the true one, war between prophetic religions is inevitable.

The simple core of a prophetic religion can be very attractive to someone who finds the rationality of materialism to be soul-less. The promise of everlasting afterlife can sound much more attractive than the pointlessness of everyday life. An increasing number of people are choosing to abandon the cosmology of materialism for religious belief, although they haven't abandoned capitalism.

The prophetic path is the path of emotion whereas materialism is the path of cold reason applied to things outside of oneself.

Mindful Emptiness

If rationality is applied also to the problems of mind, then one has the third way of rational spirituality. But it is open to the criticism that ultimately it sees the core as evanescence and emptiness, which is troubling experientially as well as logically. From experience we know that there is an inner core to ourselves that doesn't change; and if everything is transitory, then this statement should be giving lie to itself in the process.

It must use institutions to perpetuate this profoundly intellectual answer amongst the new generations. This tilts the balance of power to the intellectual elite, which leads to the concentration of power and dictatorship.

It is open to the same critique as materialism because it cannot explain what holds the transitory impressions of the mind together.

By viewing the mind on the same footing as matter, it deepens the experience of the individual and makes him see the web that connects all life. Whereas the religious person speaks of love and justice, the votary of mindful emptiness speaks of compassion.

The Fourth Way

The fourth way is the direct apprehension of reality. It takes on the world most directly, grants rational explanations for objective phenomena, yet acknowledging that the mind, by its very nature, has the capacity to comprehend the world.

It applies reason to the mind, just as the approach of mindful emptiness does, yet it doesn't stop at the logical argument since it knows that there is an unchanging substratum to experience. It acknowledges the axis of experience as the axis also of reality.

Beyond ordinary rationality, therefore, there is a mystery that cannot be measured by objective science. This mystery relates not only the individual's cognitive capacity to know but also his capacity to change and transform both himself and his environment.

The fourth way embraces reductionist logic for objects, it depends on faith in the possibility that deep experience can lead one to understanding, and it maintains that logic must be applied to the extent it can — including on the instruments of cognition — until one has reached a point beyond which lies paradox.

Materialism is about being, prophetic visions are about transportation of being to rapture upon death, mindful emptiness is enlargement of being to mind, whereas the fourth way is about becoming and creativity and joyful life.

7

Afterword

THE *sūtras* have been available on the Web for several years and this has made it possible for readers around the world to write to me with their reaction. I have been given to believe that the *sūtras* have helped in the understanding of the divide between science and spirit and, thus, have bridged it somewhat. It made them see the intuitions behind creativity and freedom in a world of order and inflexible laws.

Confronting paradox of experience and reality can either send one to despair or lead to inspirational action. My wish is for everyone to find the excitement of the journey of life, and also discover its enduring insights.

Acknowledgement

I am thankful to Georg Feuerstein, David Frawley, Abhinav Gautam, Naumi Kak, Nicholas Kazanas, Jaishree Odin, Ramakrishna Puligandla, Gopala Rao, K.L. Seshagiri Rao, Shekhar Shastri, Shruti, Sucheta, Vasuvaj, and Ananda Wood for their advice and comments.

Index